THE LORD IS MY SHEPHERD

Betsey Clark

NEW INSPIRATION FROM
FAVORITE BIBLE VERSES

The Lord Is My Shepherd

THE LORD IS MY SHEPHERD

New Inspiration From
Favorite Bible Verses

Illustrated by Betsey Clark
Selected by Mary Dawson Hughes

HALLMARK EDITIONS

The Lord Is My Shepherd

The Lord is my shepherd;
I shall not want.
He maketh me to lie down
in green pastures: he leadeth me
beside the still waters.

PSALM 23:1,2

Betsey Clark

Now faith is the substance
of things hoped for, the evidence
of things not seen.

HEBREWS 11:1

Betsey Clark

Trust in the Lord with all thine heart;
and lean not unto thine
own understanding.
In all thy ways acknowledge him,
and he shall direct thy paths.

PROVERBS 3:5-6

God is love; and he that
dwelleth in love dwelleth in God,
and God in him.

1 JOHN 4:16

Enter into his gates with
thanksgiving, and into his courts
with praise: be thankful unto him,
and bless his name.

PSALM 100:4

Betsy Clark

Betsey Clark

Consider the lilies of the field,
how they grow; they toil not,
neither do they spin.
And yet I say unto you,
That even Solomon in all his glory
was not arrayed like one of these.

MATTHEW 6:28,29

Suffer the little children
to come unto me, and forbid them not:
for of such is the kingdom of God.

MARK 10:14

If ye have faith as a grain of mustard
seed, ye shall say unto this mountain,
Remove hence to yonder place;
and it shall remove; and nothing
shall be impossible unto you.

MATTHEW 17:20

Pleasant words are as an honeycomb,
sweet to the soul, and health
to the bones.

PROVERBS 16:24

Wisdom is the principal thing;
therefore get wisdom: and with all
thy getting get understanding.
She shall give to thine head
an ornament of grace: a crown of
glory shall she deliver to thee.

PROVERBS 4:7,9

Blessed are the poor in spirit:
  for theirs is the kingdom
  of heaven.
Blessed are they that mourn:
  for they shall be comforted.
Blessed are the meek:
  for they shall inherit the earth.
Blessed are they which do hunger
  and thirst after righteousness:
  for they shall be filled.
Blessed are the merciful:
  for they shall obtain mercy.
Blessed are the pure in heart:
  for they shall see God.

MATTHEW 5:3–8

Patsey Clark

Betsey Clark

As the Father hath loved me,
so have I loved you:
continue ye in my love. . . .
This is my commandment,
That ye love one another . . . .

JOHN 15:9,12

Betsey Clark

Neither shall they say, Lo here!
or, lo there! for, behold,
the kingdom of God is within you.

LUKE 17:21

Come unto me, all ye that labour
and are heavy laden,
and I will give you rest.
Take my yoke upon you, and learn
of me; for I am meek and lowly
in heart: and ye shall find rest
unto your souls.
For my yoke is easy,
and my burden is light.

MATTHEW 11:28,30

Though I speak with the tongues of men and of angels, and have not charity, I am become as sounding brass, or a tinkling cymbal. . . .

Charity suffereth long, and is kind; charity envieth not; charity vaunteth not itself, is not puffed up . . . .

Beareth all things, believeth all things, hopeth all things, endureth all things. . . .

And now abideth faith, hope, charity, these three; but the greatest of these is charity.

1 CORINTHIANS 13:1,4,7,13

Betsey Clark

Thou shalt love the Lord thy God
with all thy heart, and with all thy
soul, and with all thy strength,
and with all thy mind;
and thy neighbor as thyself.

LUKE 10:27

Ask, and it shall be given you;
seek, and ye shall find; knock,
and it shall be opened unto you:
For every one that asketh
receiveth; and he that seeketh
findeth; and to him that knocketh
it shall be opened.

MATTHEW 7:7,8

. . . Whatsoever a man soweth,
that shall he also reap.

GALATIANS 6:7

Betsey Clark

To every thing there is a season,
and a time to every purpose
under the heaven . . . .
The thing that hath been, it is that
which shall be; and that which is
done is that which shall be done:
and there is no new thing
under the sun.

ECCLESIASTES 1:9, 3:1

And we know that all things
work together for good
to them that love God,
to them who are the called
according to his purpose.

ROMANS 8:28

Betsey Clark

This is the day which the Lord
hath made; we will rejoice
and be glad in it.

PSALM 118:24